PAPER SEAGULLS
songs and poems from the North Stand

About the author

Nic Outterside was an award-winning newspaper journalist for 28 years. He took early retirement in 2013 and is currently the proprietor of *Time is an Ocean*, the book publishing arm of **write***ahead*.
Paper Seagulls: songs and poems from the North Stand is Nic's forty-second paperback book.

PAPER SEAGULLS
songs and poems from the North Stand

Nic Outterside

Time is an Ocean Publications

Time is an Ocean Publications
An Imprint of **write***ahead*
Lonsdale Road
Wolverhampton WV3 0DY

First Printed Edition written and published
by **Time is an Ocean Publications 2022**
Text copyright © **Nic Outterside 2022**
The right of Nic Outterside to be identified as
the author of this work has been asserted by him in accordance
with the Copyright Designs and Patents Act 1988
Front cover photo © Mike Bovington
Back cover photo: © Dave Wilcock
All images within this book are copyright **Time is an Ocean
Publications** unless stated otherwise

All rights reserved
This book is sold subject to the condition that it shall not by
way of trade or otherwise be lent hired out or otherwise
circulated in any form of binding or cover other than that in
which it is published No part of this publication may be
reproduced stored in a retrieval system or transmitted in any
form or by any means (electronic mechanical photocopying
recording or otherwise) without the prior written permission of
write*ahead*

DEDICATION

To the Seagulls still flying
And the Seagulls who have flown
Once a Seagull, always a Seagull

Foreword

Football is the most tribal and all-consuming sport on our planet.

Its influence and passion spreads from Australia to Japan, Brazil, Argentina, Uruguay, central America and almost every country in Africa, to all of Russia, Europe and way beyond.

Now that passion for the *"beautiful game"* has even invaded the USA and the Middle East, pushing all other usurpers out of play.

Its human fire is stoked by the camaraderie and tribalism of its supporters who follow their chosen club until they die. But the word *"chosen"* is not actually true, because for nearly all football supporters their *"chosen"* club is usually determined by their place of birth, residence or familial influence.

But once hooked, a fan is always hooked.

In my own case, my paternal grandfather was a Geordie and die-hard Newcastle United fan. But my father had no interest in football at all. So, I guess it was left to me.

I was born in Hull, but from the age of three lived and was educated in sunny Sussex. After attending my first Brighton and Hove Albion game at the Goldstone Ground at the tender age of 11 in 1967, I was bound for life to supporting that one club.

And that loyalty and passion would not be swerved despite living most of my life in places as diverse as Huddersfield, Barnsley, Manchester,

Scotland, Tyneside and now Wolverhampton… rarely has the term *"Brighton till I die"* had such relevance.

I look to brothers and sisters I barely know, for my unity and tribal belonging. We are different ages, have different backgrounds, different political views, different tastes in music and fashion, different home towns and different education.

But we are all united by one simple fact: we support Brighton and Hove Albion and for most of us, will do until we die.

Like every other football club, our unity and camaraderie are cemented by the stadium tribalism of the chants and songs we sing in support of our club.

Some chants change and develop between the seasons, or indeed between grounds, while some are universal between clubs with the odd word tweaked to make it more personal.

And many are aimed at our bête noire – in our case our deadly rivals Crystal Palace FC.

The chants know no bounds, and there is little censorship.

But what I have done for this book is draw a firm line in the sand against anything which is racist, islamophobic, anti-semitic or homophobic. There are plenty of F bombs, crunts and wankers here but nothing to insult others by way of attacking their race, religion or sexual orientation.

However, you will find quite a few selections which defend us against the many years of homophobic abuse we have received from fans of other clubs. On most occasions our defence is quite humorous and even leaves the opposition fans chuckling.

One personal case in point which I recall was a dismal 3-0 defeat against Preston North End in 2005 at their Deepdale ground. After having one of our heroes Gary Hart sent off early on for a reckless tackle, the Preston fans in the stand to our right decided to stick the knife in, with torrents of unmitigated homophobic abuse.

Huddled in the away section, we replied in the only way we knew how... to mickey-take with overt humour and take ownership of celebrating diverse sexuality.

It started by converting our usual *"We're the right side/left side Brighton boys"* chant to: *"We're the gay side, we're the gay side, we're the gay side Brighton boys"* to then be rejoindered with *"We're the straight side, we're the straight side, we're the straight side Brighton boys"*.

And a few minutes later our 1,200 travelling fans came up with a quite brilliant *"I'd rather be a faggot than a chav"* song to the tune of Simon and Garfunkel's classic *El Condor Pasa*... even the Preston supporters laughed, although funny at the time, it is probably deemed quite un-PC today.

So, what you are holding is a book (a personal pot pourri) of songs and chants for Brighton and Hove Albion since my first game more than 55 years ago.

The selection is not censored, because the words you hear on football terraces are often not the ones you would hear or utter in Boots the Chemist, in church or indeed in front of your children or a favourite elderly aunt. The words are raw and sometimes offensive… but they are true… they comprise our united passion.

Added to this selection are a handful of personal poems about my club, which have touched some heart strings over the years.

Enjoy!

Nic Outterside
February 2022

GOSBTS

Good Ol' Sussex by the Sea
Good Ol' Sussex by the Sea
Oh, we're going up to win the cup
For Sussex by the Sea
All together now…

The Swinging Sixties

The smell of Bovril
And cigarettes
The Old Bill
And Sally suffragettes
The night time's swirling mist
Under bright lights gently kissed
The blue and white
And green so bright
Yesterday's daze in the dream smoky haze
We score
Then the roar
The mass forward surge
When bodies merge
As one
Under a floodlit sun
This game is already won
The songs and chants
The tribal dance
The love and passion
The replica fashion
No matter what the weather
The memories last forever

We love you yeah yeah yeah
We love you yeah yeah yeah
And with a goal like that
We know you should be glad

Bar Bar Bar Bar Bar Brighton
When Archie says were going to win today
It's going to happen just that way
We're going up to Division Two
We won't stop there
We'll go right through
When everything is said and done
We'll be right up there in Division One.

Pull the chain
Pull the chain
Flush em Away
Flush em Away

Black is black
The Black Prince is back
Grey was grey
When he went away
Clap clap clap

Oh my, oh my
Powney's better than Yashin
Dave Turner's better than Eusebio
And Bournemouth are in for a thrashing

I hear the sound
Of distant bums
Over there
Over there
And do they smell
Like fucking hell

Who kicks the corners?
Kit kicks the corners
Kit kicks the corners

Zigger Zagger
Zigger Zagger
Oi Oi Oi

You'll never take the North Stand
You'll never take the North Stand

Who's your father?
Who's your father?
Who's your father referee?
You ain't got one
You're a bastard
You're a bastard referee

Knees Up Mother Brown
Knees Up Mother Brown
Under the table you must go
Ee-I Ee-I Ee-I -O
If I catch you bending
I'll saw your legs right off
Knees up, knees up
Don't get the breeze up
Knees up Mother Brown
Oh, my what a rotten song
What a rotten song
What a rotten song
And what a rotten singer too

Cha Cha Cha Charlie Livesey
I'd go a million miles
For one of your goals
Oh Charlie

© **Brighton Argus**

Kit swings it in
Kit swings it in
There's gonna be a goal
When Kit swings it in

All we are saying is give us a goal

We all live at the Goldstone Ground
The Goldstone Ground
The Goldstone Ground
We all live at the Goldstone Ground
The Goldstone Ground
The Goldstone Ground

You're going home like Sandy Richardson

Bertie Mee said to Bill Shankley
Have you heard of the North Bank
Highbury?
Shanks said no
I don't think so
But I've heard of the Brighton
North Stand

Kit Napier clap clap clap clap clap
Oh Kenny Beamish
Kenny Kenny
Kenny Kenny Beamish.
Sir Norman Gall clap clap clap clap clap clap

Walk Like a Man

I was 11 years old
And the grass was green
The biggest men I'd ever seen
Through childhood eyes
The crowd was growing
Chants were sowing
Excitement flowing
Walk like a man
One day I'll
Walk like a man

I was 11 years old
And the ball was white
The scene itself was out of sight
Through childhood eyes
So much blue
The burger queue
Like a human zoo
Walk like a man
One day I'll
Walk like a man

I was 11 years old
And the ref was black
Suddenly we were on the attack
Through childhood eyes
The ball swept in
The North Stand din

We're gonna win
Walk like a man
One day I'll
Walk like a man

Loon Legs and Promotion

Brighton till I die
I'm Brighton till I die
I know I am
I'm sure I am
I'm Brighton till I die

We got Willy Willy
Irvine in our team
In our team
In our team
Willy Willy Irvine
In our team

Tiptoe through the North Stand with your boots on
Get your head kicked in
Oh, tiptoe through the North Stand with me

Tiptoe through the North Stand with a flick knife
And a sawn-off shotgun
Oh, tiptoe through the North Stand with me

We three kings of Brighton are
Kenny Beamish superstar
Sully's the greatest
Lutton's fantastic
Tra la la la la la

Shirley Temple
Shirley Temple
That's what my heart sings to me
We've got Temple
Shirley Temple
His runs make history

We took the Fratton
We walked right in
With bottles and spanners
Carving knives and hammers

To hell with Aston Villa
To hell with Notts County too
We'll fight, fight, fight for the Albion
Till we win Division Two

He's gonna break your leg
He's gonna break your leg
Oh Brian Horton
He's gonna break your leg

Gillingham fans are born illegitimate
Born illegitimate
Born illegitimate
They're just north Kent bastards

All the lads should've see us coming
Everyone was blue and white
Everyone was running
All the lads and lasses there
All with smiling faces
Going down Old Shoreham Road
To see the Brighton Aces

Look at that rocket
It's Malcolm Poskett!

One banana, two banana, three banana, four,
Five bananas make a bunch
And so do many more
Nana na na, nan na

Peter Shilton shags Alsatians
Peter Shilton shags Alsatians
He shags any dog at all

Supermac, Superstar
Walks like a woman and he wears a bra

My eyes have seen the glory of the coming of the
Lord
He plays for Brighton and Hove Albion
And his name is Peter Ward

Sully
Sully
Sully
Sully
Born is the king of Brighton

We hate Nottingham Forest
We hate Liverpool too
We hate Crystal Palace
But Brighton we love you

Knees up Brighton town
Knees up Brighton town
Top of the table we must go
Eeh aye eeh aye oh

He shot
He scored
It must be Peter Ward
Peter Ward, Peter Ward

You're gonna get your fucking head kicked in

Old boy Mullery makes your cockles glow
Slip the ball to Robbo and watch the bugger go
Norwich, Pool and Leicester give the boys a hand
And then you'll see the best team in the land!
La la la la la la la la...

You're going home in Sussex ambulance
Cos there's gonna be a nasty accident

We've got Tony, Tony, Tony, Towner on the wing

Steve Foster, my Lord, Steve Foster
Steve Foster, my Lord, Steve Foster
Steve Foster, my Lord, Steve Foster
Oh Lord, Steve Foster

You're going in the sea

You fill up our senses
Like a gallon of Harvey's
Like a packet of Woodbines
Like a good pinch of snuff
Like a good night in Brighton
Like a greasy chip butty
Oh Brighton and Hove Albion
Come thrill us again

So, here's to you Michael Robinson
Brighton loves you more than you will know
Wo wo wo

He's shagged Miss World
He's shagged Miss World
Don Shanks, never wanks
He's shagged Miss World

At no.1 was Peter Ward
At no.2 was Peter Ward
At no.3 was Peter Ward
At no.4 was Peter Ward
At no.5 was Peter Ward
At no.6 was Peter Ward
At no.7 was Peter Ward
At no.8 was Peter Ward
At no.9 was Peter Ward
At no.10 was Peter Ward
At no.11 was Peter Ward
At no.12 was Peter Ward
We all live in a Wardy Wonderland
A Wardy Wonderland
A Wardy Wonderland

© **Peter Ward**

Six foot two
Eyes of Blue
Hansie Kray is after you
La la la la, La la la la

Ian Ian Rush
Ian Rush
Ian Rush
Ian Ian Ian Rush
Ian Ian Rush
When he gets the ball
He does fuck all

If you drive a yellow Mini
You'll be shot
If you drive a yellow Mini
You'll be shot
If you drive a yellow Mini
Drive a yellow Mini
Drive a yellow Mini
You'll be shot
In the head, in the head, in the head
Like a Waldorf salad
In the head

We come from Brighton town
So, get your knickers down

Oh ah Robert Codenerrrrr

You'll never make the station
You'll never make the station.

Brighton boys we are here
We'll shag your women and drink your beer

Perry has only got one ball
His other is in the South Stand goal

We've got Stevie, Stevie
Stevie Penney on our wing
On our wing

Bring on the dustbin
Bring on the dustbin
Bring on the dustbin

Albion Albion Albion
Albion Albion Albion
Albion Albion Albion
Albion Al-Be-On

I'm forever blowing bubbles
Pretty bubbles in the air
They fly so high
They reach the sky
But like West Ham
They fade and die
Tottenham always running
Palace running too
Because the Brighton North Stand
Are running after you

Shall we sing
Shall we sing
Shall we sing a song for you

Krispies give us a song
Krispies Krispies give us a song

Hit him on the head
Hit him on the head
Hit him on the head with a baseball bat

Who ate all the pies?
Who ate all the pies?
You fat bastard
You fat bastard
You ate all the pies

We shall not be moved
We shall not be moved
Just like the team
That's gonna win Division Three
We shall not be moved

I'm a bow-legged chicken and a knock-kneed hen
We ain't lost a fight since we don't know when
We don't give a wiggle and we don't give a wank
We are the Brighton North Stand

The Goldstone Roar

Kit Napier in the wind swings the ball in
Cha Cha Cha Charlie Livesey we chanted
Big Alex rises in the fog of the night
A goal bound header he glances

Tiger Tawse races down the left wing
Behind him you can hear the North Stand sing:
"It's Brighton Hove Albion
Brighton Hove Albion FC
We're by far the greatest team
The world has ever seen"

Sully intercepts a long floated pass
Ball played wide as Mellor advances
Beamish races towards their goal
And tucks away the sweetest of chances

Tony Towner surges down the right wing
Behind him you can hear the North Stand sing:
"It's Brighton Hove Albion
Brighton Hove Albion FC
We're by far the greatest team
The world has ever seen"

Lawro takes the ball from the edge of the box
Horton signals a move they have planned
Passes to Ryan who chips it to Ward
And he scores in a Goldstone wonderland

Teddy Maybank sprints down the right wing
Behind him you can hear the North Stand sing:
"It's Brighton Hove Albion
Brighton Hove Albion FC
We're by far the greatest team
The world has ever seen"

A Jimmy Case thunderbolt bulges their net
Steve Foster ploughs through the sand
The ball swerves forward and Smith must score
But it's Robinson's shot they cannot withstand

Gary Stevens runs down the left wing
Behind him you can hear the North Stand sing:
"It's Brighton Hove Albion
Brighton Hove Albion FC
We're by far the greatest team
The world has ever seen"

There's No H in Palace

You're just a spelling mistake
Just a spelling mistake
Oi Crystal Palace
You're just a spelling mistake

We had joy we had fun we had Palace on the run
But the fun didn't last cos the bastards ran too fast
And the hills that we climbed
Was the shit they left behind

Somewhere over the Goldstone
Where Seagulls fly
If you're a Palace supporter
They'll shit in your fucking eye

I like to go a wandering along the cliffs of Dover
And if we see a Palace fan we'll kick the bastard over

I was walking down the high street
When I heard footsteps behind
It was a Palace fan
In blue and red
So, I kicked him in the goolies
And I jumped on his head
And now he is dead
Ha ha ha
Hee hee hee
I'm a Brighton boot boy
And you can't catch me

Away in a manger no crib for a bed
The little lord Jesus sat up and he said:
'We hate Palace
We hate Palace"

P-A-L-A-C-E
Stevie Coppell's got VD
With a knick knack paddy wack
Give the dog a bone
Crystal Palace
Fuck off home

When I was just little boy
I asked my mama
What shall I be
Should I be Brighton
Should I be Palace?
Here's what she said to me:
Wash your mouth out son
Go get your father's gun
We're going to Croydon
To shoot the Palace scum

Stand up if you hate Palace
Stand up if you hate Palace
Stand up if you hate Palace
Stand up if you hate Palace

If I had the wings of a sparrow
If I had the arse of a crow
I'd fly to Selhurst tomorrow
And shit on the bastards below

In your Croydon slums
In your Croydon slums
You open a dustbin for something to eat
You find a dead rat
And you think it's a treat
In your Croydon slums

I never felt more singing the blues
When Brighton win and Palace lose
Oh Brighton you've got me singing the blues.

One man went to burn (burn)
Went to burn down Selhurst (shit)
One man and his petrol bomb
Went to burn down Selhurst (shit)
Two men went to burn, etc

Hark now hear the Brighton sing
The Palace ran away
And we'll fight forever more
Because of Boxing Day

Oh I do like to be beside the seaside
Oh I do like to be beside the sea
With a lager in me hand smashing Palace in the sand
Beside the seaside beside the sea

Chim Chiminey
Chim Chiminey
Chim Chim Cheroo
We hate those bastards
In claret and blue

When I was a really little boy
My grandma bought me a cute little toy
Two palace fans hanging on a string
She told me to kick their fuckin' heads in

I went up to London just the other day
Singing, singing Brighton are the champions
I saw Malcolm Allison crying on a wall.
I said to him, what's up my friend?
He said the Palace ran again
Singing, singing Brighton are the champions

We hate Palis
We hate Palis
We are the Palis haters

Hello, hello, we are the Brighton boys
Hello, hello, we are the Brighton boys
If you are a Palace fan
Surrender or you'll die
We all follow the Albion

Build a Bonfire

No No No No No No No No No No No No No
No No No No No No No
Kurt Nogan
No No No No No No No No No No No No No
No No No No No No No
Kurt Nogan

Dickov Dickov Dickov Dickov

There's only two Kerry Mayos
There's only two Kerry Mayos

Olé Olé, Olé Olé, Nicky Rust Rust Rust

All we are saying, is give us a ground
All we are saying, is give us a ground
All we are saying, is give us a ground
All we are saying, is give us a ground
All we are saying, is give us a ground

Oh Barry Lloyd
Is unemployed
He's signing on down the dole queue
Barry Lloyd is unemployed

Build a bonfire
Build a bonfire
Put Bellotti on the top
Put Bill Archer in the middle
And burn the fucking lot
Let out the monster
Let out the monster

He's old and he's slow
Wind him up and watch him go
Les Briley, Les Briley

He wore, he wore
He wore a yellow jacket
He wore a yellow jacket
Because the orange one won't fit
And when I asked him why he wore that jacket
He said I am a steward and my head is full of shit.

Hire a Hitman
Hire a Hitman
We need a Hitman

You're not fit to
You're not fit to
You're not fit to
You're not fit to wear that shirt

You should have had the salad
You should have had the salad

Under his overcoat
Dangling free
The flasher of Wimbledon Common
Is he

If you all hate Bellotti clap your hands
If you all hate Bellotti clap your hands
If you all hate Bellotti clap your hands
If you all hate Bellotti clap your hands

They sold the ground
And now we're going down
Sack the board
Sack the board

There's only one Jeffrey Minton
And he smokes marijuana
Walking along
Smoking a bong
Walking in a Minton wonderland

And it's David Bellotti
David Bellotti MP
He's by far the biggest wanker
The World has ever seen

Briiiiighton, passion like fire
Briiiighton
Bellotti's been shown the door
Love you forever
Give up on you never
Support you for evermooooore
Briiiiighton

Johnny Crumplin Football Genius.

PC Beard my Lord, PC Beard, oh Lord, PC Beard

Sing when we're losing
Sing when we're losing
We only sing when we're losing

Failed politician
You're just a failed politician
Failed politician
You're just a failed politician

Walking down Carnaby Street
Guess who I should chance to meet
My old mate Brian Clough…
He said:
"Where's your Goldstone gone
It's a block of flats?
You're sunk"
We replied:
"No its fucking not
It's a Toys R US
You drunk."

Go left right left
Go left right left
Go pick up your steps
Go right
Go left
He shot, he scored
It must be Peter Ward
Go left right left
Go left right left
Go pick up your steps
Go right
Go left
Have you seen the Muppet Show
It's there at Selhurst Park you know
Go left right left
Go left right left
Go pick up your steps
Go right
Go left
Everywhere we go
People wanna know
Who we are
Shall we tell them
We are the famous
The famous Brighton
We are Brighton
We are Brighton
We are Brighton from the south

Come on youuuuu blueeeees

East Sussex la la la
West Sussex la la la

If you're all going to Mellor
Clap your hands
If you're all going to Mellor
Clap your hands

Do your neighbours know you're a crook?
Do your neighbours know you're a crook?
Do your neighbours know you're a crook?
Do your neighbours?
Yes, do your neighbours?
Do your neighbours know you're a crook?

Time to blame the referee

Let's pretend we scored a goal
Let's pretend we scored a goal

Sack In the Morning,
You'll Get the Sack
In the Morning

You missed a goal
Too long getting a pie
Finding your cock
Undoing your fly
You fat bastard
You fat bastard
You missed a goal

We are Brighton
We are Brighton
We are Brighton from the South

Drinking Cider

Drinking cider
To life and more
In a Hereford pub
Passing round the ready rub
We've been to the bottom
Of Bellotti's scheme
But we are still alive
To move on and dream
No more sorrow
We believe in tomorrow
Okay I'll have some whisky
And more wine
This feeling's fine
I can sense another song
But we are Brighton
And Hove Albion
And now we all move on

A Theatre of Trees

© Brighton Argus

We're Dick Knight's blue and white army
We're Dick Knight's blue and white army
We're Dick Knight's blue and white army
We're Dick Knight's blue and white army
We're Dick Knight's blue and white army

Oh, Chris McPhee oh Chris McPhee
Won't you score a goal for me

Micky Adams' Blue and White Army
Micky Adams' Blue and White Army

Posh Spice is a slapper
She really is a tart
And when she's shagging Beckham
She dreams of Gary Hart.

Mark McGhee
Mark McGhee
Drinking pints of whisky
Mark McGhee

You're too ugly to be gay
You're too ugly to be gay

When the ball hits the net like a fuckin' Exocet
It's Zamora
There's no one there
There's no one there
There's no one there
There's no one there.

Michael Kuipers
He's a former Dutch marine
A former Dutch marine
A former Dutch marine

Does your boyfriend know you're here?
He's over there
He's over there

Hold me closer, Fran Sandanza
You came all the way from Dundee
Your hair is very lovely
I can't believe we got you for free
Hold me closer, Fran Sandanza
You'll love playing by the sea
You scored the winner against Oldham
If you were gay would you marry me?

Since you came to Withdean
Our midfield is the best
You've helped pick the pieces up
We're so happy
That we've got Radostin Kishishev
Radostin, Radostin, Radostin
Kish-i-shev

See him dribbling
See him passing
See him dancing
Such a star
Kazenga, Kazenga, Kazenga
LuaLua

You're Jocks, and you know you are
You're Jocks, and you know you are

Walk like a chicken that's got no head
Walk like a cockney with a broken leg

What the fucking
What the fucking
What the fucking hell was that?

Albion Albion
We're the famous Brighton and Hove Albion
We are Blue, we are White
We are fucking dynamite.

Shit ground, no fans
Shit ground, no fans
Shit ground, no fans
Shit ground, no fans

We filled your stadium
We filled your stadium
We filled your stadium
We filled your stadium

If you go down to the woods today
Be sure of a big surprise
Coz today's the day that Jeremy joined the skinheads

Is this a library?
Is this a library?
Is this a library?
Is this a library?
Sshhh sshhh

When the ball hits the net
It's not Shearer or Cole
It's Zamora

Up North
It's fucking grim up North
It's fucking grim up North
Up North
It's fucking grim up North

One song!
You've only got one song!
You've only got one song!

I'd Rather Be a Faggot than a Chav
Yes I would
If I could
I surely would

Is this a fire drill?
Is this a fire drill?
Is this a fire drill?
Is this a fire drill?

We're the east side
We're the east side
We're the east side Brighton boys
We're the west side
We're the west side
We're the west side Brighton boys

We're the straight side
We're the straight side
We're the straight side Brighton boys
We're the gay side
We're the gay side
We're the gay side Brighton boys

Can you see us holding hands?
Can you see us holding hands?

We've got Dicker
We've got Cox
We've got Dunk
Our team is full
Our team is full
Our team is full of spunk
Albion

We have tiny Cox
We have tiny Cox

Adam El-abd do do do do do do
Adam El-abd do do do do do do
Adam El-abd do do do do do do

You're not a big club anymore
You're not a big club anymore
You're not a big club anymore
You're not a big club anymore

One – Nil to the Nancy boys

We've got massive Wood
We've got massive Wood

Can we play you?
Can we play you?
Can we play you every week?
Can we play you every week?

Your father is your brother
Your sister is your mother
You all fuck one another
You're the Ipswich family

You're supposed to
You're supposed to
You're supposed to be at home
You're supposed to be at home

Going down
Going down
So are we
So are we

Sing when you're fishing
You only sing when you're fishing

Stand up if you want Falmer
Stand up if you want Falmer
Stand up if you want Falmer
Stand up if you want Falmer

Build It and They Will Come

© Dave Wilcock

When he plays for Brighton
He runs
He runs
He runs
I just can't get enough
I just can't get enough

Loft, Loft will tear you apart again

He scores with his face
He scores with his face
Inigo Calderon
He scores with his face

We're fucking brilliant
We're fucking brilliant
We're fucking brilliant
We're fucking brilliant

De, de, de, de, Craig Mackail-Smith
De, de, de, de, Craig Mackail-Smith
De, de, de, de, Craig Mackail-Smith
De, de, de, de, Craig Mackail-Smith

He's one of our own
He's one of our one
Lewis Dunk
He's one of our own

We've got a German
A big fucking German
The Lion sleeps tonight
We've got a German
A big fucking German
Uwe Hunemeier
Will make you look like shite

David Stockdale's Magic
He doesn't wear a hat
He could have stayed at Fulham
But he said go fuck that
He saves them with his left hand
He saves them with his right
And when we win promotion
We'll sing this song all night

Who's that man from Argentina
Who's that man we all adore
Leonardo is his name
And he scores a goal a game
And we don't mention Murray anymore

Oscar Garcia
He drinks sangria
He came from Barca
To bring us joy
He's got more stubble than Barney Rubble
So please don't take our Oscar away

We're on our way
We're on our way
To the Premier League
We're on our way
How we get there
I don't know
How we get there
I don't care
All I know that Brighton's on their way

We've got Knockaert
We've got Knockaert
Anthony Knockaert
I just don't think you understand
He only cost two mill
And he's better than Ozil
We've got Anthony Knockaert

We've got a big Pole in our goal
We've got a big Pole in our goal

We can see you
We can see you
We can see you sneaking out
We can see you sneaking out

He's not got much hair
But we don't care
You'd better fit a new lock
Eat a stick of Brighton Rock
Cos he scores with his cock
Glenn Murray

West stand West stand give us a song
West Stand West Stand give us a song
Come On You Blues from the West Stand

He plays on the left
He plays on the right
That boy Barnes
Makes Palace look shite

Oh Stevie Sidwell
You are the love of my life,
Oh Stevie Sidwell
I'd let you shag my wife,
Oh Stevie Sidwell
I want ginger hair too!

Oh Neal Maupay
Ooh ahh
I wanna know ow ow ow ow
How you scored that goal

There's a Starman
Running Down the right
His name is Tariq Lamptey
And he's fucking dynamite

He scores at the end
He always scores at the end
Oh Neal Maupay
He scores at the end

Big Dan Burn
He's long and he's tall
He sleeps in the kitchen
With his feet in the hall

Marco Cucurella
The hottest thing from Alella
Marco, Marco Cucurella
Our wing back with the el pelo
It's Marco Cucurella

Oh Tariq Lamptey
He signed from Chelsea
Plays for Brighton
He's our Number 2
Running down the right wing
As fast as lightning
Oh Tariq Lamptey
How we love you

No-one can Stop Knockaert

The moon is rising over Ashton Gate
I feel the breath of a storm
Something's gonna happen tonight
You go inside and stay warm,
Sidwell will score from 50 yards
I can see it in his stare
And they'll raise Knocky's shirt up high
To show how much they care

There's no-one who can stop Knockaert
There's no-one who can stop Knockaert
There's no-one who can stop Knockaert
You, you, you, you
Yeah, you can't stop Knockaert

Remember that time in the city of steel
When the Wednesday hoodoo crashed
Knocky mesmerised the full back
The Owls knew that they'd been thrashed,
No one thought it would happen like this
When Norwich came to town
Murray helped himself in a game of bliss
And Knocky chipped their clown

There's no-one who can stop Knockaert
There's no-one who can stop Knockaert
There's no-one who can stop Knockaert
You, you, you, you

Yeah, you can't stop Knockaert

A low strike against Rotherham and Reading
The winner against Huddersfield
Just like a party at a wedding
When Knocky made Forest yield,
Some say football is important
More than your seat in the stand
But those words they are transportant
As together we hold his hand

There's no-one who can stop Knockaert
There's no-one who can stop Knockaert
There's no-one who can stop Knockaert
You, you, you, you
Yeah, you can't stop Knockaert

MFIS

Armpit offside
Free kick was wide
Goal is disallowed
Jeers are loud
Cameras zoom
There ain't no room
Ref has spoken
Silence broken
Open goal
Green glory hole
Twelve yards
Red card
Sent off
Gotta cough
Not fit for the shirt
The chant must hurt
Heroes and villains
Riders and pillions
Home and away
United in grey
Zigger and zagger
Scissor and swagger
Promotion
Demotion
Not a penalty
Mistaken identity
On pitch review
Clear for the few

Decision from afar
But
Sometimes modern football
All goes too VAR

Legends of the Ball

Bobby Farrell and Zamora
Are legends of the fall
Bert Stephens and Kit Napier
Both knew where to put the ball
Peter Ward and Glenn Murray
Were raised to hero status
Their skill and natural talent
Supreme strikers and creators
But behind and alongside them
There were also many others
They belong in our collective memories
As legends and Albion brothers

Albion Sundown

Your shoes, they were bought in Boohoos
Your dress is from Taiwan
Your bedding's from Malaysia
Your ruck sack's from Amazon
That skirt you wear comes from the Philippines
And the phone you use is a Lumia Grey
It was put together in Chengdu
By a girl making seven Yuan a day

Well, it's sundown on the Goldstone
West Pier and the Corn Exchange
A train ride to the Amex
Where no-one thinks it's strange
Thirty-six quid for a football match
You play their game and pay
Sure was a good idea
Until greed got in the way

Well, your dress is made in Suzhou
And all our cars are from Japan
Your silk scarf was bought in Primark
The Fat Face jeans from Pakistan
All the furniture, it says "Made in Brazil"
Where a woman, she slaved for sure
Bringing home 60 pence a day to a family of twelve
You know, that's a lot of money to her

Well, it's sundown on the Goldstone
The ABC and the Corn Exchange
A train ride to the Amex
Where no-one thinks it's strange
Thirty-six quid for a football match
You play their game and pay
Sure was a good idea
Until greed got in the way

You know, capitalism is above the law
Because *"It don't count unless it sells"*
When it costs too much to build it at home
You just build it cheaper somewhere else
And the job that you used to have
They gave it to somebody in El Salvador
Football sold out to Sky TV
And now it's dying like a dinosaur

Well, it's sundown on the Goldstone
Moth Records and the Corn Exchange
A train ride to the Amex
Where no-one thinks it's strange
Thirty-six quid for a football match
You play their game and pay
Sure was a good idea
Until greed got in the way

Democracy doesn't rule the world
That's something you need to understand
This world is ruled by bankers
Who use politics as a sleight-of-hand
From Preston Park to King Alfred Baths
That's a lot of property indeed
And a man's got to do what he has to do
When he's got a hungry mouth to feed

Well, it's sundown on the Goldstone
St Albans Church and the Corn Exchange
A train ride to the Amex
Where no-one thinks it's strange
Thirty-six quid for a football match
You play their game and pay
Sure was a good idea
Until greed got in the way

Fans United Will Never Be Defeated

Ken Richardson's fire
Stoked the Doncaster ire
It only took a spark
To ignite his moment in the dark

They can't understand
In their money-grabbing hands
When they try to steal our game
They are all the fuckin same
We will not be tamed and seated
Fans united together
Will never be defeated

Bill Archer made a killing
From his crooked Goldstone shilling
But the battling Seagulls now fly
Under a blue and white sky

They can't understand
In their money-grabbing hands
When they try to steal our game
They are all the fuckin same
We will not be tamed and seated
Fans united together
Will never be defeated

Alex Hamilton's wrecking ball
Swung the Racecourse call
As the evil ball came down
Wrexham's own fans saved their ground

They can't understand
In their money-grabbing hands
When they try to steal our game
They are all the fuckin same
We will not be tamed and seated
Fans united together
Will never be defeated

Roland Duchatelet's sleight of hand
United the Valley stand
The fans then dealt their own CARD
And they cleared him from their yard

They can't understand
In their money-grabbing hands
When they try to steal our game
They are all the fuckin same
We will not be tamed and seated
Fans united together
Will never be defeated

Karl Oyston sued football fans for fun
But his regime is now undone
Under the famous Blackpool lights
Defeated by the Tangerine Knights

They can't understand
In their money-grabbing hands
When they try to steal our game
They are all the fuckin same
We will not be tamed and seated
Fans united together
Will never be defeated

Acknowledgements and thanks

Brian Allcorn
Alana Baker
Andy Baker
Ken Baverstock
Mike Bovington
Ash Bradley
Alan Budgen
Neil Burchell
Martyn Burke
Mick Burns
John Caffrey
Rory Clarke
John Cleeves
Joe Cocozza
Steve Cowdry
Paul Cornwell
Michael Cull
Jason Dance
Martin Denny
Neil English
Jason Fenner
Chris Frean
Adam Goodchild
Ray Green
Paul and Judy Gunn
Phil Hanmer
Cliff Hart
Ian Hart
David Olly Holledge
Adam Holmes
Chris Huet

Paul Hunter
John Hewitt
Keith Ives
Peter Jenkins
Roby Jones
Rob Lamb
John Lawson
Simon Levenson
Martin Loz Lawrence
Ingram Losner
Matthew McWalter
Gary Martin
Paul Martin
Richard Murphy
Kris Mole
Gill Outterside
Neil Peters
Russ Poore
Guy Preston
Nigel Rowe
Andrew Shall
Phil Shelley
Wayne Smith
Malcolm Stuart
Mick Sutton
Steve Tennyson
Rosemary Ticehurst
David Trenner
Neil Underhill
Steve Underhill
Ricky William Wainwright
Mark Walker
Dave Wilcock

Alan Willard
Andy Wooldridge
Chris Worrall
James Cory Wright

About the Author

Paper Seagulls: Songs and Poems from the North Stand is written and edited by Nic Outterside, and published by his UK independent publishing house ***Time is an Ocean Publications***.

Nic has been a fervent supporter of Brighton & Hove Albion since watching his first game at the Goldstone Ground in September 1967.

His previous books about the Albion: ***Death In Grimsby*** and ***Wet Socks and Dry Bones*** both became Amazon best-sellers in 2019 and 2021 respectively.

Nic is also an award-winning journalist and creative author, who over 37 years has worked across all forms of media, including radio, magazines, newspapers, books and online.

Among more than a dozen awards to his name are *North of England Daily Journalist of the Year, Scottish Daily Journalist of the Year, Scottish Weekly Journalist of the Year* and a special award for investigative journalism.

In 1994, 53 MPs signed an Early Day Motion in the UK House of Commons praising Nic's research and writing.

In 2016, Nic was awarded an honorary doctorate in written journalism.

Paper Seagulls: Songs and Poems from the North Stand is his 42nd published book.

Available from all Amazon portals and Waterstones
Price: £9.99

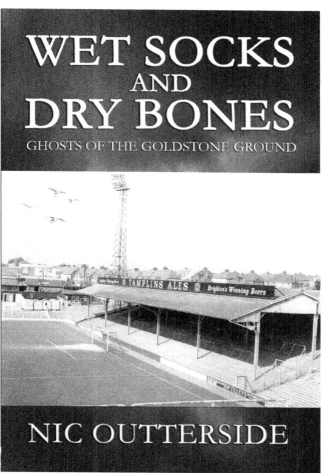

Available from all Amazon portals and Waterstones
Price: £11.99

Books by Time is an Ocean Publications

The Hill - Songs and Poems of Darkness and Light
Another Hill - Songs and Poems of Love and Theft
Asian Voices
Asian Voices - the Director's Cut
Blood in the Cracks
Don't Look Down
Luminance - Words for a World Gone Wrong
Death in Grimsby
Bones
Hot Metal – Poems from the Print Room
Poets Don't Lie
Contacts
The Man's a Tart
Western Skies
Reality Cornflakes
A Moon Magnetized This Screeching Bird
The Arbitrary Fractals of an Oracle
Dissect My Fragile Brain
Sonnets
Spiced Dreams and Scented Schemes
Minotaur and Other Poems
An Alpine State of Mind
Blue Note Poems
Love Like a Rose
Under the Weight of Blue
Echoes and Stardust
Wet Socks and Dry Bones
In Pursuit of Dragonflies
An Escape to Stay
Pharmacy
Addled Petals

Baker's Dozen
When the Party's Over
Pulling Mussels
Spilling Earl Grey Tea on an Oriental Rug
Moonbeam-Sentinels/Sunbeam-Forgettance
Alliteration to Ziplock Zippies
Paper Seagulls

Printed in Great Britain
by Amazon